# THIS NATION
# UNDER
# GOD

*A book of aids to*
*worship in the*
*Bicentennial year 1976*

*Prepared by*
*The Committee on the Observance of the Bicentennial*

*in cooperation with*
*The Standing Liturgical Commission*

*and recommended for use by*
*The Presiding Bishop*
*and*
*The President of the House of Deputies*
*of the General Convention of*
THE EPISCOPAL CHURCH IN THE UNITED STATES OF AMERICA

The Seabury Press
815 Second Avenue
New York, N. Y. 10017

Printed in the United States of America

Library of Congress Catalog Number 76-378

ISBN 0-8164-78090

Produced by Seabury Professional Services

THE RESOLUTION adopted in the General Convention of 1973 at Louisville concerning the observance, in 1976, of the two hundredth anniversary of the signing of the Declaration of Independence:

*Whereas,* The Bicentennial of the Declaration of Independence and the founding of the United States of America will be observed in 1976; and

*Whereas,* The observance of these events reminds us of the closely related development of the Episcopal Church as an independent branch of the Anglican Communion in the new nation and of its contributions to the establishment of the nation's principles and traditional commitments; and

*Whereas,* The Presiding Bishop has appointed a Committee on Observance of the Bicentennial; now be it

RESOLVED,

1. That this 64th General Convention of the Episcopal Church hereby endorse and commend to every Diocese and congregation in the United States appropriate participation and co-operation with such ecumenical, national, and local bicentennial observances as may be proposed, and that the American Churches in Europe be encouraged to participate fully in the celebration of the 200th Anniversary of the Declaration of Independence;
2. That emphasis be placed in these observances not only on past history, but primarily upon the opportunities in the present to affirm and extend the promise of ''liberty and justice for all'';
3. That special attention and study be devoted to the contributions made in past and present to our national and religious life by Native Americans, Afro-Americans, Oriental Americans, and other minority groups; and be it further

*RESOLVED,* That this General Convention recommend that the years 1974 and 1975 be a time for planning and preparation for such bicentennial observances, nationally and in each Diocese and Congregation; that a series of events be planned for 1976, with the suggestion that the season of Lent and the period near Independence Day and Thanksgiving Day be appropriately observed as occasions of penitence for our national sins, of celebration of our national achievements, of re-affirmation of our duties as citizens and of the obligations of government to respect the right to peaceful and orderly criticism and dissent, and of a celebration of hope for the nation "conceived in liberty" and committed to the principle of "government of the people, by the people, and for the people."

The three parts of this booklet are offered to the church as suggestions of ways to implement the provisions of this resolution as far as services of worship are concerned. The Committee on the Observance of the Bicentennial hopes that each parish and diocese will hold several observances during the year 1976, and that the contents of this booklet will be of assistance in planning them.

## *The Committee on the Observance of the Bicentennial*

The Rev. Dr. John B. Coburn, *Chairman*
The Rev. C. Fitz Allison
The Rt. Rev. John M. Burgess
Mr. Hodding Carter, III
The Very Rev. Richard Coombs
Mrs. Priscilla B. Dewey
The Rev. Robert Golledge
Mr. Augustus T. Graydon
Dr. Clifford P. Morehouse
Mr. Dennis Sun Rhodes
The Very Rev. Francis Sayre
Dr. Cynthia Wedel
The Rev. William J. Wolf
The Rev. Canon Stewart Wood, Jr.
The Rev. John H.M. Yamazaki

Dr. V. Nelle Bellamy—*Consultant*

The Rev. Page S. Bigelow—*Staff*
The Rev. Everett W. Francis—*Staff*

# *Prayers*

## *FOR THE BICENTENNIAL*

O Almighty and everlasting God, your power calls the nations of the world into being, your Providence sustains them, your righteousness judges them: Give us your grace, we pray, that we may celebrate the Bicentennial of this nation in a manner that will please you. Fill our hearts with thankfulness for the gifts and achievements which have blessed us during the years past, and for your many and great mercies toward us. Bring us to repentance for the sins and wrongs which we have done or from which we profit, and give us strength to amend our ways. Above all, enable us so to dedicate ourselves to your just and loving purposes that we may labor for the freedom and well-being of all people, following the example of our Lord and Savior Jesus Christ; to whom with you and the Holy Spirit, be all might, majesty, dominion and power, now and for ever.                    AMEN

## *FOR OUR COUNTRY*

Almighty God, who hast given us this good land for our heritage; We humbly beseech thee that we may always prove ourselves a people mindful of thy favor and glad to do thy will. Bless our land with honorable industry, sound learning, and pure manners. Save us from violence, discord, and confusion; from pride and arrogance, and from every evil way. Defend our liberties, and fashion into one united people the multitudes brought hither out of many kindreds and tongues. Endue with the spirit of wisdom those to whom in thy Name we entrust the authority of government, that there may be justice and peace at home, and that, through obedience to thy law, we may show forth thy praise among the nations of the earth. In the time of prosperity, fill our hearts with thankfulness, and in the day of trouble, suffer not our trust in thee to fail; all which we ask through Jesus Christ our Lord.          AMEN

# Table of Contents

part I

# *Propers for Three Special Occasions*

The Bicentennial Resolution commends to the Church three occasions for special worship during the Bicentennial Year. One, in Lent, is to be observed as a day of national repentance. The First Sunday in Lent would be an appropriate date. The second, on or near Independence Day, is to be observed as a day of national thanksgiving. The third, on or near Thanksgiving Day, is to be observed as a day of national rededication.

In this section are found suggested propers for these three special observances. Three sets of psalms and lessons are provided for each of the three days. Any set may be used for Morning or Evening Prayer, or the Eucharist, at the discretion of the Minister. The first set is recommended for the principal service of the day. Extra psalms and lessons should simply be omitted. If the Sunday Morning Service of 1776 is used (Part III), it will be necessary to choose two sets of propers for the "accumulated services" customary at that time.

Some of these psalms and lessons are appointed in the 1928 Book of Common Prayer or in the Draft Proposed Book for corresponding occasions. Other selections are newly provided for the Bicentennial celebration.

Verses in parentheses designate possible shortening or lengthening of psalms or lessons.

Two canticles are provided for each of the three days. The text is that of the Draft Proposed Book. Other canticles from the Book of Common Prayer or from Authorized Services 1973 may also be used. Suggested hymns are from the Hymnal 1940.

# A Day of National Repentance

(FOR THE FIRST SUNDAY IN LENT, OR SOME OTHER
APPROPRIATE DAY IN LENT.)

## THE COLLECT[1]

*(Traditional language)*  Almighty God, by whose guiding hand this nation was set upon the paths of justice and liberty; By thy mercy forgive us, we beseech thee, our many failures and refusals to walk in thy ways. Renew a right spirit amongst us; and bring us again to such a sense of thy righteous will, that, following it, we may show forth thy glory to the nations and live with them in thy peace; through Jesus Christ our Lord.                                                AMEN

*(Contemporary language)*  Almighty God, by whose guiding hand this nation was set upon the paths of justice and liberty; By your mercy forgive us, we pray, our many failures and refusals to walk in your ways. Renew a right spirit among us; and bring us again to such a sense of your righteous will, that, following it, we may show forth your glory to the nations and live with them in your peace; through Jesus Christ our Lord.                                                AMEN

[1] Dr. Coburn

## PSALMS AND LESSONS

I. *Psalm 85:1–7 (13)*
 *Isaiah 24:4–13*          Earth mourns transgressions against God.
 *Hebrews 13:1–6*         Ethical obligations under God's covenant.
 *Matthew 25:31–45*      ". . . the least of these my brethren . . ."

II. *Psalm 78:1–12*
 *Jeremiah 7:1–15*        False confidence in religious observances
 *Revelation 18:10b-17*   The Fall of Babylon
 *Luke 21:25–33*          Signs of the coming Kingdom of God.

*III. Psalm 80*

| | |
|---|---|
| *Daniel 9:3–19* | Daniel confesses national disobedience. |
| *I Peter 2:11–17* | ". . . Fear God. Honor the emperor . . ." |
| *John 11:47–52* | That one should die and that the nation should not perish |

---

PROPER PREFACE OF LENT

---

## Suggestions

It would be appropriate to use the Litany at this service, either in procession at the beginning, or in place of the regular intercessions at the Eucharist, or in the customary place after the Third Collect at Morning or Evening Prayer. On this occasion, the full text should be read, including all the material between the Lord's Prayer and the concluding collect.

In place of the General Confession, the Litany of National Repentance may be used.

## A LITANY OF NATIONAL REPENTANCE

O God, our merciful and righteous Judge, we confess to you that we as a nation have often disobeyed your will and betrayed our vision of liberty and justice for all people.

Forgive us.

We have worshipped the power and wealth which your bounty and forbearance have made possible for us, but we have often neglected to worship you, the one true God.

Forgive us.

We have often abused and oppressed those weaker than ourselves.

Forgive us.

Some of our forebears who acted for us and in our name have dealt cruelly and dishonorably with the native Americans whose land this once was.

Forgive us.

Some enslaved countless thousands of black persons, and many profited from their bondage.

Forgive us.

We have boasted of justice and often created injustice.

Forgive us.

We have boasted of freedom and often supported tyranny.

Forgive us.

We have boasted of plenty, and often allowed neighbors to want.

Forgive us.

We have boasted of honor, and often tolerated lawlessness in public and private life.

Forgive us.

And we have supposed that you did not regard our disobedience or care about our sin.

Forgive us.

MINISTER AND PEOPLE:    Hear our prayer, O Lord, for you are patient and full of compassion. Have mercy upon us, have mercy upon your people who turn to you with contrite and penitent hearts. Spare us our just deserts, and save us from hopeless confusion; and according to your great mercy, forgive us all our sins, for the sake of your blessed Son, our Savior, Jesus Christ.        AMEN

(If a priest or bishop is present, he should pronounce Absolution.)

## SUITABLE CANTICLE
FOLLOWING THE OLD TESTAMENT LESSON

A Song of Penitence, Kyrie Pantokrator
Prayer of Manasseh, 1-2, 4, 6-7, 11-15

O Lord and Ruler of the hosts of heaven,*
    God of Abraham, Isaac, and Jacob,
    and of all their righteous offspring:
You made the heavens and the earth,*
    with all their vast array.

All things quake with fear at your presence;*
 they tremble because of your power.
But your merciful promise is beyond all measure;*
 it surpasses all that our minds can fathom.
O Lord, you are full of compassion,*
 long-suffering, and abounding in mercy.
You hold back your hand;*
 you do not punish as we deserve.
In your great goodness, Lord, you have promised
  forgiveness to sinners,*
 that they may repent of their sin and be saved.
And now, O Lord, I bend the knee of my heart,*
 and make my appeal, sure of your gracious
  goodness.
I have sinned, O Lord, I have sinned,*
 and I know my wickedness only too well.
Therefore I make this prayer to you:*
 forgive me, Lord, forgive me.
Do not let me perish in my sin,*
 nor condemn me to the depths of the earth.
For you, O Lord, are the God of those who repent,*
 and in me you will show forth your goodness.
Unworthy as I am, you will save me,
 in accordance with your great mercy,*
 and I will praise you without ceasing all the days of
  my life.
For all the powers of heaven sing your praises,*
 and yours is the glory to ages of ages.  AMEN

## SUITABLE CANTICLE
### FOLLOWING THE NEW TESTAMENT LESSON

The Song of Mary, Magnificat
Luke 1:46–55

 My soul proclaims the greatness of the Lord,
  my spirit rejoices in God my Savior,*
  for he has looked with favor on his lowly servant.
 From this day all generations will call me blessed:*

the Almighty has done great things for me,
    and holy is his Name.
He has mercy on those who fear him*
    in every generation.
He has shown the strength of his arm,*
    he has scattered the proud in their conceit.
He has shown the strength of his arm,*
    he has scattered the proud in their conceit.
He has filled the hungry with good things,*
    and the rich he has sent away empty.
He has come to the help of his servant Israel,*
    for he has remembered his promise of mercy,
The promise he made to our fathers,*
    to Abraham and his children for ever.

Glory to the Father, and to the Son, and to the Holy
    Spirit:*
    as it was in the beginning, is now, and will be for
    ever.

AMEN

Additional Canticles may be found in *Authorized Services*

The Second Song of Isaiah (Quaerite Dominum)
A Song of Praise (Benedictus es)
The Song of Simeon (Nunc dimittis)
The Song of the Redeemed (Magna et mirabilia)

## SUITABLE HYMNS

147 God of Our Fathers, Known of Old
435 Dear Lord and Father of Mankind
518 Judge Eternal, Throned in Splendor
519 Once to Every Man and Nation
521 O God of Earth and Altar
522 Lord Christ, When First Thou Cam'st to Men
523 God the Omnipotent
532 Father Eternal
536 Turn Back, O Man

# A Day of National Thanksgiving

## THE COLLECT[1]

*(Traditional language)*  Most gracious God, whose Word is the source of our life and whose Kingdom is the fulfillment of our hope: By thy creating and redeeming love, grant us such grateful hearts that we may continually thank thee for the many blessings which we have received from thy hands during past years; and make us, we beseech thee, faithful stewards of thy bounty, serving thee by sharing it with others; through thy Son, Jesus Christ our Lord, who with thee and the Holy Spirit liveth and reigneth now and for ever.        AMEN

*(Contemporary language)*  Most gracious God, your Word is the source of our life and your Kingdom is the fulfillment of our hope; By your creating and redeeming love, give us grateful hearts to thank you for the many blessings which we have received in past years; and make us, we pray, faithful stewards of your good gifts, serving you by sharing them with others; through your Son, Jesus Christ our Lord, who with you and the Holy Spirit lives and reigns now and for ever.        AMEN

[1] Bishop Allin

## PSALMS AND LESSONS

| | |
|---|---|
| I. Psalm 65. (9–14) | |
| Psalm 145. (1–13) | |
| Deuteronomy 8.1–11 | |
| 17–20 | Remember the way God has led us |
| Philippians 4.4–9 | Rejoice in the Lord always! |
| Matthew 6.25–33 | Do not be anxious. |

II. *Psalm 107.1–9*
    *Deuteronomy 26.1–11*    Offering with thanksgiving to the
                                   Lord of History.
    *James 1.16–25*    Every good gift is from above
    *Luke 8.4–15*    On bringing forth good fruit with patience

III. *Psalm 117, 118*
    *Isaiah 35*    The wilderness blooms
    *Revelation 21.1–4*
            *22–27*    The new creation
    *Matthew 4.1–11*    The conquest of temptation

---

## PROPER PREFACE OF TRINITY

---

## *Suggestions*

For Intercessions on this occasion a Litany of Thanksgiving or the Thanksgiving for the Nation may be used.

# *A LITANY OF THANKSGIVING*

Let us give thanks to God our Father for all his gifts so freely bestowed upon us: For the beauty and wonder of his creation, in earth and sky and sea,

We thank you, Lord.

For all that is gracious in the lives of men and women, revealing the image of Christ,

We thank you, Lord.

For our daily food and drink, our homes and families, and our friends,

We thank you, Lord.

For minds to think, and hearts to love, and hands to serve,

We thank you Lord.

For health and strength to work, and leisure to rest and play,

We thank you, Lord.

For the brave and courageous, who are patient in suffering and faithful in adversity,

We thank you, Lord.

For all valiant seekers after truth, liberty and justice,

We thank you, Lord.

For the communion of saints, in all times and places,

We thank you, Lord.

Above all, let us give thanks for the great mercies and promises given to us in Christ Jesus, our Lord;

To him be praise and glory, with the Father and the Holy Spirit, now and for ever.                                                   AMEN

OR

## FOR THE NATION

Almighty God, giver of all good things:
We thank you for the natural majesty and beauty of this land.
They restore us, though we often destroy them.

Heal us.

We thank you for the great resources of this nation. They make us rich, though we often exploit them.

Forgive us.

We thank you for the men and women who have made this country strong. They are models for us, though we often fall short of them.

Inspire us.

We thank you for the torch of liberty which has been lit in this land. It has drawn people from every nation, though we have often hidden from its light.

Enlighten us.

We thank you for the faith we have inherited in all its rich variety. It sustains our life, though we have been faithless again and again.

Renew us.

Help us, O Lord, to finish the good work here begun. Strengthen our efforts to blot out ignorance and prejudice, and to abolish poverty and crime. And hasten the day when all our people, with many voices in one united chorus, will glorify your holy Name.                    AMEN

## SUITABLE CANTICLE
### FOLLOWING THE OLD TESTAMENT LESSON

A Song of Creation, Benedicite, omnia opera Domini
Song of the Three Young Men, 35-65

One or more sections of this Canticle may be used. Whatever the selection, it begins with the Invocation and concludes with the Doxology.

## INVOCATION

Glorify the Lord, all you works of the Lord,*
    praise him and highly exalt him for ever.
In the firmament of his power, glorify the Lord.*
    praise him and highly exalt him for ever.

### I  The Cosmic Order

Glorify the Lord, you angels and all powers of the Lord,*
    O heavens and all waters above the heavens.
Sun and moon and stars of the sky, glorify the Lord,*
    praise him and highly exalt him for ever.

Glorify the Lord, every shower of rain and fall of dew,*
    all winds and fire and heat.
Winter and summer, glorify the Lord,*
    praise him and highly exalt him for ever.

Glorify the Lord, O chill and cold,*
    drops of dew and flakes of snow,
Frost and cold, ice and sleet, glorify the Lord.*
    praise him and highly exalt him for ever.

Glorify the Lord, O nights and days,*
   O shining light and enfolding dark.
Storm clouds and thunderbolts, glorify the Lord,*
   praise him and highly exalt him for ever.

## II  The Earth and its Creatures

Let the earth glorify the Lord,*
   praise him and highly exalt him for ever.
Glorify the Lord, O mountains and hills,
   and all that grows upon the earth,*
   praise him and highly exalt him for ever.

Glorify the Lord, O springs of water, seas, and streams,*
   O whales and all that move in the waters.
All birds of the air, glorify the Lord,*
   praise him and highly exalt him for ever.

Glorify the Lord, O beasts of the wild,*
   and all you flocks and herds.
O men and women everywhere, glorify the Lord,*
   praise him and highly exalt him for ever.

## III  The People of God

Let the people of God glorify the Lord,*
   praise him and highly exalt him for ever.
Glorify the Lord, O priests and servants of the Lord,*
   praise him and highly exalt him for ever.

Glorify the Lord, O spirits and souls of the righteous,*
   praise him and highly exalt him for ever.
You that are holy and humble of heart, glorify the Lord,*
   praise him and highly exalt him for ever.

## DOXOLOGY

Let us glorify the Lord: Father, Son, and Holy Spirit;*
   praise him and highly exalt him for ever.
In the firmament of his power, glorify the Lord,*
   praise him and highly exalt him for ever.

## *SUITABLE CANTICLE*
FOLLOWING THE NEW TESTAMENT LESSON

A Song to the Lamb, Dignus es
Revelation 4:11; 5:9–10, 13

> Splendor and honor and kingly power*
>> are yours by right, O Lord our God,
> For you created everything that is,*
>> and by your will they were created and have their being,
>
> And yours by right, O Lamb that was slain,*
>> for with your blood you have redeemed for God,
> From every family, language, people, and nation,*
>> a kingdom of priests to serve our God.
>
> And so, to him who sits upon the throne,*
>> and to Christ the Lamb,
> Be worship and praise, dominion and splendor,*
>> for ever and for evermore.

Additional Canticles may be found in *Authorized Services*
Te Deum
Jubilate

## *APPROPRIATE HYMNS*

> 141  My Country 'Tis of Thee
> 142  The Star-Spangled Banner
> 143  God of Our Fathers, Whose Almighty Hand
> 146  God Bless Our Native Land
> 506  Land of Our Birth, We Pledge to Thee
> 520  Rejoice, O Land, in God Thy Might
> 523  God, the Omnipotent
> 524  God of Grace, and God of Glory
> 525  O Day of God, Draw Nigh
> 528  O God of Love, O King of Peace
> 529  Lord God of Hosts, Whose Mighty Hand
> 538  God is Working His Purpose Out

# A Day of National Rededication

## THE COLLECT

*(Traditional language)*   Lord God Almighty, in whose name the founders of this country won liberty for themselves and us, and lit the torch of freedom for nations then unborn: Grant, we beseech thee, that we and all the people of this land may have grace to maintain these liberties in righteousness and peace; through Jesus Christ our Lord.   AMEN

*(Contemporary language)*   Lord God Almighty, in whose name the founders of this country won liberty for themselves and us, and lit the torch of freedom for nations then unborn: Grant that we and all the people of this land may have grace to maintain these liberties in righteousness and peace; through Jesus Christ our Lord.   AMEN

## PSALMS AND LESSONS

*I  Psalm 66*
  *Psalm 72*
  *Deuteronomy 30.8–20*      I have set before you this day life and
          OR                      good . . .
  *Joshua 24.14–18*        "Choose you this day whom you will serve."
  *Ephesians 6.10–17*       The whole armor of God
  *Mark 12.13–17*          Caesar's and God's

*II Psalm 145*
  *Micah 4.1–5*            Swords beaten to ploughshares.
          OR
  *Deuteronomy 10.17–21*   God executes justice,
  *Hebrews 11.8–16*        The city whose maker and builder is God.
  *Matthew 5.43–48*        Love your enemies

21

*III Psalm 67*

    *Isaiah 26.1–8*                 The righteous nation which keeps faith

    *Romans 13.1–10*            All authority comes from God

         OR

    *Revelation 21.1–7*          The new Jerusalem

    *John 18.33–37*               "My kingship is not of this world."

---

PROPER PREFACE OF ADVENT

---

## Suggestions

Appropriate intercessions, particularly with a Second Rite Eucharist, would consist of a group of prayers: one for the Church, for our Country, for Social Justice, and for Peace which may be found in *Authorized Services*.

## SUITABLE CANTICLE
FOLLOWING THE OLD TESTAMENT LESSON

The Second Song of Isaiah, Quaerite Dominum
Isaiah 55:6—11

Seek the Lord while he wills to be found,*
    call upon him when he draws near.
Let the wicked forsake their ways,*
    and the evil ones their thoughts;
And let them turn to the Lord, and he will have
        compassion,*
    and to our God, for he will richly pardon.
For my thoughts are not your thoughts,*
    nor your ways my ways, says the Lord.
For as the heavens are higher than the earth,*
    so are my ways higher than your ways,
    and my thoughts than your thoughts.
For as rain and snow fall from the heavens,*
    and return not again, but water the earth,
Bringing forth life and giving growth,*
    seed for sowing and bread for eating,

So is my word that goes forth from my mouth,*
    it will not return to me empty;
But it will accomplish that which I have purposed,*
    and prosper in that for which I sent it.

Glory to the Father, and to the Son, and to the Holy
    Spirit;* as it was in the beginning, is now, and will
    be for ever.                                        AMEN

## SUITABLE CANTICLE
FOLLOWING THE NEW TESTAMENT LESSON

The Song of Simeon, Nunc dimittis
Luke 2:29–32

    Lord, now lettest thou thy servant depart in peace,*
        according to thy word;
    For mine eyes have seen thy salvation,*
        which thou hast prepared before the face of all
        people,
    To be a light to lighten the Gentiles,*
        and to be the glory of thy people Israel.

    Glory to the Father, and to the Son, and to the Holy
        Spirit;* as it was in the beginning, is now, and will
        be for ever.                                    AMEN

The Song of Simeon, Nunc dimittis
Luke 2:29–32

    Lord, you now have set your servant free*
        to go in peace as you have promised;
    For these eyes of mine have seen the Savior,*
        whom you have prepared for all the world to see:
    A Light to enlighten the nations,*
        and the glory of your people Israel.

    Glory to the Father, and to the Son, and to the Holy
        Spirit;* as it was in the beginning, is now, and will
        be for ever.                                    AMEN

Additional Canticles may be found in *Authorized Services*

First Song of Isaiah (Ecce, Deus)
A Song to the Lamb (Dignus es)
Te Deum
Jubilate

## *APPROPRIATE HYMNS*

137  Come, Ye Thankful People, Come
138  We Plow the Fields and Scatter
139  Praise God, from Whom All Blessings Flow
140  Praise to God, Immortal Praise
144  Lord God, We Worship Thee
148  O God, Beneath Whose Guiding Hand
276  Now Thank We All Our God
277  From All That Dwell Below the Skies
278  All People that on Earth Do Dwell
279  Praise to the Lord, the Almighty
281  Joyful, Joyful, We Adore Thee
282  Praise, My Soul, the King of Heaven

part II

# A Te Deum of Thanksgiving for the Bicentennial

# A Te Deum of Thanksgiving for the Bicentennial

One of the traditional forms of expressing thanksgiving to God on an occasion of national rejoicing is the singing of a Te Deum. Special settings of the Te Deum have been commissioned for the Bicentennial celebration, and it would be fitting to sing them when this service is used.

It may be used for any Bicentennial observance except the three provided for Part I. It is hoped that it will be found acceptable for ecumenical purposes.

# A Te Deum of Thanksgiving for the Bicentennial

(TRADITIONAL LANGUAGE)

A Psalm or Hymn may be sung during the entrance of the Ministers. The People being assembled, and all standing, the officiating Minister says,

Blessed be God: Father, Son, and Holy Spirit.
PEOPLE: And blessed be his Kingdom, now and forever. AMEN.
MINISTER: Righteousness exalteth a nation.
PEOPLE: The Lord is our God: we will serve him.
MINISTER: The Lord be with you.
PEOPLE: And with thy spirit.
MINISTER: Let us pray.

Most gracious God, source of all life and all goodness: By thy creating and redeeming love, give us, we beseech thee, such grateful hearts, that we may be faithful stewards of thy good gifts, and ever give thanks to thee in sharing them with others; through thy Son Jesus Christ our Lord, who with thee and the Holy Spirit liveth and reigneth now and forever.    AMEN

OR THIS

Lord God Almighty, in whose Name the founders of this country won liberty for themselves and for us, and lit the torch of freedom for nations then unborn: Grant, that we and all the people of this land may have grace to maintain our liberties in righteousness and peace; through Jesus Christ our Lord.    AMEN

Then may be read one of the following or some other suitable lesson:
    Deuteronomy 8.1–11; 17–20
    Joshua 24.14–25
    Mark 12.13–17
    Matthew 25.31–45

## *TE DEUM LAUDAMUS*

We praise thee, O God; we acknowledge thee to be the
        Lord.
All the earth doth worship thee, the Father everlasting.
To thee all Angels cry aloud:
The Heavens and all the Powers therein;
To thee Cherubim and Seraphim continually do cry,
Holy, Holy, Holy, Lord God of Sabaoth;
Heaven and earth are full of the Majesty of thy glory.
The glorious company of the Apostles praise thee.
The goodly fellowship of the Prophets praise thee.
The noble army of Martyrs praise thee.
The holy Church throughout all the world
        doth acknowledge thee;
The Father of an infinite Majesty;
Thine adorable, true, and only Son;
Also the Holy Ghost the Comforter.

Thou art the King of Glory, O Christ.

Thou art the everlasting Son of the Father.
When thou tookest upon thee to deliver man,
    thou didst humble thyself to be born of a Virgin.
When thou hadst overcome the sharpness of death,
    thou didst open the Kingdom of Heaven to all
    believers.
Thou sittest at the right hand of God,
    in the glory of the Father.

We believe that thou shalt come to be our Judge.
We therefore pray thee, help thy servants,
    whom thou hast redeemed with thy precious blood.
Make them to be numbered with thy Saints,
    in glory everlasting.

MINISTER: The Lord be with you.
PEOPLE: And with thy spirit.
MINISTER: Let us pray.

Our Father, who art in heaven, hallowed be thy Name, thy Kingdom come, thy will be done, on earth as it is in heaven. Give us this day our daily bread. And forgive us our trespasses, as we forgive those who trespass against us. And lead us not into temptation, but deliver us from evil. For thine is the Kingdom, and the power, and the glory, for ever and ever. AMEN.

MINISTER: Show us thy mercy, O Lord:
PEOPLE: And grant us thy salvation.
MINISTER: Clothe thy ministers with righteousness:
PEOPLE: Let thy people sing with joy.
MINISTER: Give peace, O Lord, in all the world:
PEOPLE: For only in thee can we live in safety.
MINISTER: Lord, keep this nation under thy care:
PEOPLE: And guide us in the way of justice and truth.
MINISTER: Let thy way be known upon earth:
PEOPLE: Thy saving health among all nations.
MINISTER: Let not the needy, O Lord, be forgotten:
PEOPLE: Nor the hope of the poor be taken away.
MINISTER: Create in us clean hearts, O God:
PEOPLE: And sustain us with thy Holy Spirit.

The following, or other suitable prayers, are then said.

## *FOR THE NATION*

Lord God Almighty, who has made all the peoples of the earth for thy glory, to serve thee with freedom and peace; grant to the people of our country a zeal for justice, and the strength of forbearance, that we may use our liberty in accordance with thy gracious will; through Jesus Christ our Lord, who liveth and reigneth with thee and the Holy Spirit, one God, for ever and ever.                                                    AMEN

## *FOR SOCIAL JUSTICE*

Almighty God, who hast created man in thine own image: Grant us grace fearlessly to contend against evil, and to make no peace with oppression; and, that we may reverently use our freedom, help us to employ it in the maintenance of justice among men and nations, to the glory of thy holy Name; through Jesus Christ our Lord.          AMEN

## *FOR PEACE*

Almighty God, from whom all thoughts of truth and peace proceed: Kindle, we pray thee, in the hearts of all men the true love of peace; and guide with thy pure and peaceable wisdom those who take counsel for the nations of the earth, that in tranquillity thy kingdom may go forward, until the earth is filled with the knowledge of thy love; through Jesus Christ our Lord.                                              AMEN

## *FOR GOD'S MERCY*

Almighty God, the fountain of all wisdom, who knowest our necessities before we ask, and our ignorance in asking: We beseech thee to have compassion upon our infirmities; and those things which for our unworthiness we dare not, and for our blindness cannot ask, mercifully give us, for the worthiness of thy Son, Jesus Christ our Lord, who liveth and reigneth with thee and the Holy Spirit, one God, now and for ever. AMEN

*Other prayers may be added if desired, concluding with the General Thanksgiving and a Blessing.*

# A Te Deum of Thanksgiving for the Bicentennial

(CONTEMPORARY LANGUAGE)

A Psalm or Hymn may be sung during the entrance of the Ministers.

The People being assembled, and all standing, the officiating Minister says,

Blessed be God: Father, Son, and Holy Spirit.

PEOPLE: And blessed be his Kingdom, now and forever.     AMEN

MINISTER: Righteousness exalts a nation.

PEOPLE: The Lord is our God: we will serve him.

MINISTER: The Lord be with you.

PEOPLE: And also with you.

MINISTER: Let us pray.

Most gracious God, source of all life and all goodness: By your creating and redeeming love, we pray, give us such grateful hearts that we may be faithful stewards of your good gifts, and ever give thanks to you in sharing them with others; through your Son, Jesus Christ our Lord, who with you and the Holy Spirit lives and reigns now and forever.   AMEN

OR THIS

Lord God Almighty, in whose Name the founders of this country won liberty for themselves and for us, and lit the torch of freedom for nations then unborn: Grant that we and all the people of this land may have grace to maintain our liberties in righteousness and peace; through Jesus Christ our Lord.                                          AMEN

Then may be read one of the following or some other suitable lesson:

    Deuteronomy 8.1–11; 17–20

    Joshua 24.14–25

    Mark 12.13–17

    Matthew 25.31–45

## *TE DEUM LAUDAMUS*

You are God: we praise you;
You are the Lord: we acclaim you;
You are the eternal Father:
All creation worships you.
To you all angels, all the powers of heaven,
Cherubim and Seraphim, sing in endless praise:
>    Holy, Holy, Holy Lord, God of power and might,
>    heaven and earth are full of your glory.
The glorious company of apostles praise you.
The noble fellowship of prophets praise you.
The white-robed army of martyrs praise you.
Throughout the world the holy Church acclaims you:
>    Father, of majesty unbounded,
>    your true and only Son, worthy of all worship,
>    and the Holy Spirit, advocate and guide.

You, Christ, are the king of glory,
>    the eternal Son of the Father.
When you became man to set us free
You did not shun the Virgin's womb.
You overcame the sting of death
>    and opened the Kingdom of heaven to all believers.
You are seated at God's right hand in glory,
We believe that you will come and be our judge.
>    Come then, Lord, and help your people,
>    bought with the price of your own blood,
>    and bring us with your saints
>    to glory everlasting.

MINISTER: The Lord be with you.
PEOPLE: And also with you.
MINISTER: Let us pray.

Our Father in heaven, hallowed be your Name,
>    your kingdom come,
Your will be done,
>    on earth as in heaven.
Give us today our daily bread.

Forgive us our sins
   as we forgive
      those who sin against us.
Save us from the time of trial
   and deliver us from evil.
For the kingdom, the power,
   and the glory are yours,
      now and for ever. AMEN.

MINISTER: Show us your mercy, O Lord:
PEOPLE: And grant us your salvation.
MINISTER: Clothe your ministers with righteousness:
PEOPLE: Let your people sing with joy.
MINISTER: Give peace, O Lord, in all the world:
PEOPLE: For only in you can we live in safety.
MINISTER: Lord, keep this nation under your care:
PEOPLE: And guide us in the way of justice and truth.
MINISTER: Let your way be known upon earth:
PEOPLE: Your saving health among all nations.
MINISTER: Let not the needy, O Lord, be forgotten:
PEOPLE: Nor the hope of the poor be taken away.
MINISTER: Create in us clean hearts, O God:
PEOPLE: And sustain us with your Holy Spirit.

The following, or other suitable prayers, are then said.

## FOR THE NATION

Lord God Almighty, you have made all the peoples of the earth for your glory, to serve you in freedom and in peace: Give to the people of our country a zeal for justice, and the strength of forbearance, that we may use our liberty in accordance with your gracious will; through Jesus Christ our Lord, who lives and reigns with you and the Holy Spirit, one God, for ever and ever.                                    AMEN

## FOR SOCIAL JUSTICE

Almighty God, who created man in your own image; Grant us grace fearlessly to contend against evil, and to make no peace with oppression; and, that we may reverently use our freedom, help us to employ it in the maintenance of justice among men and nations, to the glory of your holy Name; through Jesus Christ our Lord.    AMEN

## FOR PEACE

Almighty God, from whom all thoughts of truth and peace proceed: Kindle in the hearts of all men the true love of peace; and guide with your pure and peaceable wisdom those who take counsel for the nations of the earth, that in tranquillity your kingdom may go forward, until the earth is filled with the knowledge of your love; through Jesus Christ our Lord.    AMEN

## FOR GOD'S MERCY

Almighty God, the fountain of all wisdom, since you know our necessities before we ask, and our ignorance in asking: Have compassion on our weakness; and mercifully give us those things which in our unworthiness we dare not, and for our blindness we cannot ask, for the worthiness of your Son Jesus Christ our Lord, who lives and reigns with you and the Holy Spirit, one God; now and forever.    AMEN

*Other prayers may be added if desired, concluding with the General Thanksgiving and a Blessing.*

part III

# The Sunday Morning
# Service in 1776

# The Sunday Morning Service in 1776

A Church of England service on a Sunday morning in 1776 would have been in many respects similar to the twentieth century services of the American Episcopal Church with which we are familiar, but in some respects it would have been quite different.

## THE ENGLISH BOOK OF 1662

There was a different Prayer Book. The Book then in use was the English Book of Common Prayer of 1662, still the authorized book in England. The fundamental pattern of its services closely resembles that of the American Book of 1928, which we use. Many, if not most, of the words would be the same. But we would quickly notice certain unfamiliar features. A strongly penitential note pervades it, for example, set at once by the selection of opening sentences at Morning Prayer, so different from the ones we know, and by the required use of the Ten Commandments at Holy Communion. Moreover, the services permit considerably less variety. There are fewer canticles at Morning and Evening Prayer from which to make a choice; and there is no permission to omit the General Confession. In the Communion Service, the Summary of the Law is not included either as an optional substitute for the Ten Commandments or as an addition to them, and the reading of a lengthy exhortation is always required. These features tend to make the services not only less flexible, but also considerably longer.

## ACCUMULATED OR COMBINED SERVICES

An even more striking difference lies in the way the book was used in 1776. For the previous two hundred years (and for more than one hundred thereafter), beginning with a directive from Archbishop Grindal in 1571, the Prayer Book service on a normal Sunday morning consisted of Morning Prayer, as far as the Third Collect (for Grace); then the Litany (which until 1928 was required by rubric to be read on Sundays, Wednesdays and Fridays); and then either Ante-Communion, concluding, after the Prayer for the Whole State of Christ's Church, with one or more of the collects printed at the end of the service and the blessing, or else the entire Communion Service. During the colonial period Holy Communion was usually celebrated in most parishes three or four times a year, although in 1776 the number of parishes with monthly celebrations, of which there had been some in the colonies from an early date, was growing under the impact of the Evangelical (Methodist) revival. With a sermon at the indicated place after the Nicene Creed, the whole Sunday morning service would probably have lasted about two hours.

## ORNAMENTS AND VESTMENTS

Colored silk hangings, reference to the Holy Table as an altar, and colored stoles or eucharistic vestments for the priest, did not become common in Anglican worship until well into the nineteenth century. The customary usage in colonial times would have been quite simple. Holy Communion was celebrated on the "holy table", a regular wooden table with legs. At communion time it was covered with a fair linen cloth. There may have been nothing else. There was often an additional covering, the so-called "Laudian cloth", an ample tablecloth-like covering, frequently of red velvet, reaching to the floor on four sides. There was no cross, and frequently no candles.

Generally the celebrant wore a black preaching gown. . . . like those still worn by many Protestant clergy. In a number of places, however, he would have worn a surplice, (in the long full style which is beginning to be seen again), up to the metrical psalm before the sermon. At that point he would have exchanged the surplice for the gown, and after the sermon changed to his surplice.

Most colonial churches had "two-decker" or "three-decker" pulpits, with prayer desk, lectern, and pulpit combined into one structure. From its various levels, Minister and clerk would have read Morning Prayer and the Litany.

## NORTH-END CELEBRATIONS

The Communion service, however, was read from the "north" end of the Holy Table—the left end as seen from the congregation. The priest faced "south"; the people looked at his profile. The position is still fairly common in England, although it disappeared in this country during the earlier years of this century.

The custom of celebrating from the north end arose during the sixteenth century. The English Book of 1552, published at the high-tide of the Reformation, assumed that medieval altars had either been torn out of churches or had fallen into disuse; and that Communion would be celebrated at a table placed lengthwise between the choir-stalls. The priest was directed to stand on the north, because this position would put him on the middle of a long side. Those who stayed for communion would sit in the choir-stalls facing him. Some sixty or seventy years later, tables were returned to the east wall; but the rubric remained, and priests continued to stand at the north-end of the table even in the restored place. This position has at least the advantage of allowing the congregation to witness the manual acts of the priest.

## MUSIC

In 1776, there was no official hymn book for the Church of England. Tate and Brady's metrical psalms were popular  Only a few of the hymns of this period have survived the test of time and gained inclusion in the 1940 Hymnal.

The following Tate and Brady hymns are in the 1940 Hymnal

    85 Jesus Christ is Ris 'n Today
    390 O 'Twas a Joyful Sound to Hear
    439 My Soul With Patience Waits
    450 As Pants the Hart for Cooling Streams

*Songs for Liturgy and More Hymns and Spiritual Songs* contains two hymns by William Billings, an American composer, of the period: H-31 Through North and South and East and West, and H-39 When Jesus Wept.

# The order for
# *MORNING PRAYER,*
# *daily throughout the year*

¶ *At the beginning of Morning Prayer the Minister shall read with a loud voice some one or more of these Sentences of the Scriptures that follow. And then he shall say that which is written after the said Sentences.*

WHEN the wicked man turneth away from his wickedness that he hath committed, and doeth that which is lawful and right, he shall save his soul alive.          *Ezek.* xviii. 27.

I acknowledge my transgressions, and my sin is ever before me.
*Psal.* li. 3.

Hide thy face from my sins, and blot out all mine iniquities.
*Psal.* li. 9.

The sacrifices of God are a broken spirit: a broken and a contrite heart, O God, thou wilt not despise.
*Psal.* li. 17.

Rend your heart, and not your garments, and turn unto the Lord your God: for he is gracious and merciful, slow to anger, and of great kindness, and repenteth him of the evil.
*Joel* ii. 13.

To the Lord our God belong mercies and forgivenesses, though we have rebelled against him: neither have we obeyed the voice of the Lord our God, to walk in his laws which he set before us.          *Dan.* ix. 9, 10.

O Lord, correct me, but with judgement; not in thine anger, lest thou bring me to nothing.
*Jer.* x. 24. *Psal.* vi, l.

Repent ye; for the Kingdom of heaven is at hand.          *St. Matth.* iii. 2.

I will arise, and go to my father, and will say unto him, Father, I have sinned against heaven, and before thee, and am no more worthy to be called thy son.          *St. Luke* xv. 18, 19.

Enter not into judgement with thy servant, O Lord; for in thy sight shall no man living be justified.
*Psal.* cxliii. 2.

If we say that we have no sin, we deceive ourselves, and the truth is not in us: but, if we confess our sins, he is faithful and just to forgive us our sins, and to cleanse us from all unrighteousness.          1 *St. John* i. 8, 9.

DEARLY beloved brethren, the Scripture moveth us in sundry places to acknowledge and confess our manifold sins and wickedness; and that we should not dissemble nor cloke them before the face of Almighty God our heavenly Father; but confess them with an humble, lowly, penitent, and obedient heart; to the end that we may obtain forgiveness of the same, by his infinite goodness and mercy. And although we ought at all times humbly to acknowledge our sins before God; yet ought we most chiefly so to do, when we assemble and meet together to render thanks for the great benefits that we have received at his hands, to set forth his most worthy praise, to hear his most holy Word, and to ask those things which are requisite and necessary, as well for the body as the soul. Wherefore I pray and beseech you, as many as are here present, to accompany me with a pure heart, and humble voice, unto the throne of the heavenly grace, saying after me;

¶ *A general Confession to be said of the whole Congregation after the Minister, all kneeling.*

ALMIGHTY and most merciful Father; We have erred, and strayed from thy ways like lost sheep. We have followed too much the devices and desires of our own hearts. We have offended against thy holy laws. We have left undone those things which we ought to have done; And we have done those things which we ought not to have done; And there is no health in us. But thou, O Lord, have mercy upon us, miserable offenders. Spare thou them, O God, which confess their faults. Restore thou them that are penitent; According to thy promises declared unto mankind in Christ Jesu our Lord. And grant, O most merciful Father, for his sake; That we may hereafter live a godly, righteous, and sober life, To the glory of thy holy Name. Amen.

¶ *The Absolution, or Remission of sins, to be pronounced by the Priest alone, standing; the people still kneeling.*

ALMIGHTY God, the Father of our Lord Jesus Christ, who desireth not the death of a sinner, but rather that he may turn from his wickedness, and live; and hath given power, and commandment, to his Ministers, to declare and pronounce to his people, being penitent, the Absolution and Remission of their sins: He pardoneth and absolveth all them that truly repent, and unfeignedly believe his holy Gospel. Wherefore let us beseech him to grant us true repentance, and his holy Spirit, that those things may please him, which we do at this present; and that the rest of our life hereafter may be pure, and holy; so that at the last we may come to his eternal joy; through Jesus Christ our Lord.

¶ *The people shall answer here, and at the end of all other prayers,* Amen.

¶ *Then the Minister shall kneel, and say the Lord's Prayer with an audible voice; the people also kneeling, and repeating it with him, both here, and wheresoever else it is used in Divine Service.*

OUR Father, which art in heaven, Hallowed be thy Name. Thy kingdom come. Thy will be done in earth, As it is in heaven. Give us this day our daily bread. And forgive us our trespasses, As we forgive them that trespass against us. And lead us not into temptation; But deliver us from evil: For thine is the kingdom, The power, and the glory, For ever and ever. Amen.

¶ *Then likewise he shall say,*

O Lord, open thou our lips.
ANSWER. And our mouth shall shew forth thy praise.

PRIEST. O God, make speed to save us.

ANSWER. O Lord, make haste to help us.

¶ *Here all standing up, the Priest shall say,*

Glory be to the Father, and to the Son: and to the Holy Ghost;

ANSWER. As it was in the beginning, is now, and ever shall be: world without end. Amen.

PRIEST. Praise ye the Lord.

ANSWER. The Lord's Name be praised.

¶ *Then shall be said or sung this Psalm following: except on* Easter-Day, *upon which another Anthem is appointed; and on the Nineteenth day of every Month it is not to be read here, but in the ordinary Course of the Psalms.*

*Venite, exultemus Domino.*
Psal. XCV.

O C O M E , let us sing unto the Lord: let us heartily rejoice in the strength of our salvation.

Let us come before his presence with thanksgiving: and shew ourselves glad in him with Psalms.

For the Lord is a great God: and a great King above all gods.

In his hand are all the corners of the earth: and the strength of the hills is his also.

The sea is his, and he made it: and his hands prepared the dry land.

O come, let us worship, and fall down: and kneel before the Lord our Maker.

For he is the Lord our God: and we are the people of his pasture, and the sheep of his hand.

To day if ye will hear his voice,

harden not your hearts: as in the provocation, and as in the day of temptation in the wilderness;

When your fathers tempted me: proved me, and saw my works.

Forty years long was I grieved with this generation, and said: It is a people that do err in their hearts, for they have not known my ways.

Unto whom I sware in my wrath: that they should not enter into my rest.

Glory be to the Father, and to the Son: and to the Holy Ghost;

As it was in the beginning, is now, and ever shall be: world without end. Amen.

¶ *Then shall follow the Psalms in order as they are appointed. And at the end of every Psalm throughout the Year, and likewise at the end of* Benedicite, Benedictus, Magnificat, *and* Nunc dimitis, *shall be repeated,*

Glory be to the Father, and to the Son: and to the Holy Ghost;

ANSWER. As it was in the beginning, is now, and ever shall be: world without end. Amen.

¶ *Then shall be read distinctly with an audible voice the First Lesson, taken out of the Old Testament, as is appointed in the Calendar, except there be Proper Lessons assigned for that day: He that readeth so standing and turning himself, as he may best be heard of all such as are present. And after that, shall be said or sung, in* English, *the Hymn called* Te Deum Laudamus, *daily throughout the Year.*

¶ *Note, That before every Lesson the Minister shall say,* Here beginneth such a Chapter, *or* Verse of such a Chapter, of such a Book: *And after every Lesson,* Here endeth the First, *or* the Second Lesson.

*Te Deum Laudamus.*

WE PRAISE thee, O God: we acknowledge thee to be the Lord.

All the earth doth worship thee: the Father everlasting.

To thee all Angels cry aloud: the Heavens, and all the Powers therein.

To thee Cherubin, and Seraphin: continually do cry,

Holy, Holy, Holy: Lord God of Sabaoth;

Heaven and earth are full of the Majesty: of thy Glory.

The glorious company of the Apostles: praise thee.

The goodly fellowship of the Prophets: praise thee.

The noble army of Martyrs: praise thee.

The holy Church throughout all the world: doth acknowledge thee;

The Father: of an infinite Majesty;

Thine honourable, true: and only Son;

Also the Holy Ghost: the Comforter.

Thou art the King of Glory: O Christ.

Thou art the everlasting Son: of the Father.

When thou tookest upon thee to deliver man: thou didst not abhor the Virgin's womb.

When thou hadst overcome the sharpness of death: thou didst open the Kingdom of Heaven to all believers.

Thou sittest at the right hand of God: in the Glory of the Father.

We believe that thou shalt come: to be our Judge.

We therefore pray thee, help thy servants: whom thou hast redeemed with thy precious blood.

Make them to be numbered with thy Saints: in glory everlasting.

O Lord, save thy people: and bless thine heritage.

Govern them: and lift them up for ever.

Day by day: we magnify thee;

And we worship thy Name: ever world without end.

Vouchsafe, O Lord: to keep us this day without sin.

O Lord, have mercy upon us: have mercy upon us.

O Lord, let thy mercy lighten upon us: as our trust is in thee.

O Lord, in thee have I trusted: let me never be confounded.

¶ *Or this Canticle,*

*Benedicite, omnia Opera.*

O ALL YE Works of the Lord, bless ye the Lord: praise him, and magnify him for ever.

O ye Angels of the Lord, bless ye the Lord: praise him, and magnify him for ever.

O ye Heavens, bless ye the Lord: praise him, and magnify him for ever.

O ye Waters that be above the Firmament, bless ye the Lord: praise him, and magnify him for ever.

O all ye Powers of the Lord, bless ye the Lord: praise him, and magnify him for ever.

O ye Sun, and Moon, bless ye the Lord: praise him, and magnify him for ever.

O ye Stars of Heaven, bless ye the Lord: praise him, and magnify him for ever.

O ye Showers, and Dew, bless ye the Lord: praise him, and magnify him for ever.

O ye Winds of God, bless ye the Lord: praise him, and magnify him for ever.

O ye Fire and Heat, bless ye the Lord: praise him, and magnify him for ever.

O ye Winter and Summer, bless ye the Lord: praise him, and magnify him for ever.

O ye Dews, and Frosts, bless ye the Lord: praise him, and magnify him for ever.

O ye Frost and Cold, bless ye the Lord: praise him, and magnify him for ever.

O ye Ice and Snow, bless ye the Lord: praise him, and magnify him for ever.

O ye Nights, and Days, bless ye the Lord: praise him, and magnify him for ever.

O ye Light and Darkness, bless ye the Lord: praise him, and magnify him for ever.

O ye Lightnings, and Clouds, bless ye the Lord: praise him, and magnify him for ever.

O let the Earth bless the Lord: yea, let it praise him, and magnify him for ever.

O ye Mountains, and Hills, bless ye the Lord: praise him, and magnify him for ever.

O all ye Green Things upon the Earth, bless ye the Lord: praise him, and magnify him for ever.

O ye Wells, bless ye the Lord: praise him, and magnify him for ever.

O ye Seas, and Floods, bless ye the Lord: praise him, and magnify him for ever.

O ye Whales, and all that move in the Waters, bless ye the Lord: praise him, and magnify him for ever.

O all ye Fowls of the Air, bless ye the Lord: praise him, and magnify him for ever.

O all ye Beasts, and Cattle, bless ye the Lord: praise him, and magnify him for ever.

O ye Children of Men, bless ye the Lord: praise him, and magnify him for ever.

O let Israel bless the Lord: praise him, and magnify him for ever.

O ye Priests of the Lord, bless ye the Lord: praise him, and magnify him for ever.

O ye Servants of the Lord, bless ye the Lord: praise him, and magnify him for ever.

O ye Spirits and Souls of the Righteous, bless ye the Lord: praise him, and magnify him for ever.

O ye holy and humble Men of heart, bless ye the Lord: praise him, and magnify him for ever.

O Ananias, Azarias, and Misael, bless ye the Lord: praise him, and magnify him for ever.

Glory be to the Father, and to the Son: and to the Holy Ghost;

As it was in the beginning, is now, and ever shall be: world without end. Amen.

¶ *Then shall be read in like manner the Second Lesson, taken out of the New Testament. And after that, the Hymn following; except when that shall happen to be read in the Chapter for the Day, or for the Gospel on* St. John Baptist's *Day.*

*Benedictus.* St. Luke i. 68.

BLESSED be the Lord God of Israel: for he hath visited, and redeemed his people;

And hath raised up a mighty salvation for us: in the house of his servant David;

As he spake by the mouth of his holy Prophets: which have been since the world began;

That we should be saved from our enemies: and from the hands of all that hate us;

To perform the mercy promised to our forefathers: and to remember his holy Covenant;

To perform the oath which he sware to our forefather Abraham: that he would give us;

That we being delivered out of the hand of our enemies: might serve him without fear;

In holiness and righteousness before him: all the days of our life.

And thou, Child, shalt be called the Prophet of the Highest: for thou shalt go before the face of the Lord to prepare his ways;

To give knowledge of salvation unto his people: for the remission of their sins,

Through the tender mercy of our God: whereby the day-spring from on high hath visited us;

To give light to them that sit in darkness, and in the shadow of death: and to guide our feet into the way of peace.

Glory be to the Father, and to the Son: and to the Holy Ghost;

As it was in the beginning, is now, and ever shall be: world without end. Amen.

¶ *Or this Psalm,*

*Jubilate Deo.* Psal. c.

O B E joyful in the Lord, all ye lands: serve the Lord with gladness, and come before his presence with a song.

Be ye sure that the Lord he is God: it is he that hath made us, and not we ourselves; we are his people, and the sheep of his pasture.

O go your way into his gates with thanksgiving, and into his courts with praise: be thankful unto him, and speak good of his Name.

For the Lord is gracious, his mercy is everlasting: and his truth endureth from generation to generation.

Glory be to the Father, and to the Son: and to the Holy Ghost;

As it was in the beginning, is now, and ever shall be: world without end. Amen.

¶ *Then shall be sung or said the Apostles' Creed by the Minister and the people, standing: except only such days as the Creed of* Saint Athanasius *is appointed to be read.*

I B E L I E V E in God the Father Almighty, Maker of heaven and earth:

And in Jesus Christ his only Son our Lord, Who was conceived by the Holy Ghost, Born of the Virgin Mary, Suffered under Pontius Pilate, Was crucified, dead, and buried, He descended into hell; The third day he rose again from the dead, He ascended into heaven, And sitteth on the right hand of God the Father Almighty; From thence he shall come to judge the quick and the dead.

I believe in the Holy Ghost; The holy Catholick Church; The Communion of Saints; The Forgiveness of sins; The Resurrection of the body, And the life everlasting. Amen.

¶ *And after that, these Prayers following, all devoutly kneeling; the Minister first pronouncing with a loud voice,*

The Lord be with you.
ANSWER. And with thy spirit.
MINISTER. Let us pray.
Lord, have mercy upon us.
*Christ, have mercy upon us.*
Lord, have mercy upon us.

¶ *Then the Minister, Clerks, and people, shall say the Lord's Prayer with a loud voice.*

O U R Father, which art in heaven, Hallowed be thy Name. Thy kingdom come. Thy will be done in earth, As it is in heaven. Give us this day our daily bread. And forgive us our trespasses, As we forgive them that trespass against us. And lead us not into temptation; But deliver us from evil. Amen.

¶ *Then the Priest standing up shall say,*

O Lord, shew thy mercy upon us.
ANSWER. And grant us thy salvation.
PRIEST. O Lord, save the King.
ANSWER. And mercifully hear us when we call upon thee.
PRIEST. Endue thy Ministers with righteousness.
ANSWER. And make thy chosen people joyful.
PRIEST. O Lord, save thy people.
ANSWER. And bless thine inheritance.
PRIEST. Give peace in our time, O Lord.

ANSWER. Because there is none other that fighteth for us, but only thou, O God.
PRIEST. O God, make clean our hearts within us.
ANSWER. And take not thy holy Spirit from us.

¶ *Then shall follow three Collects; the first of the Day, which shall be the same that is appointed at the Communion; the second for Peace; the third for Grace to live well. And the two last Collects shall never alter, but daily be said at Morning Prayer throughout all the Year, as followeth; all kneeling.*

*The second Collect, for Peace.*
O  G O D , who art the author of peace and lover of concord, in knowledge of whom standeth our eternal life, whose service is perfect freedom; Defend us thy humble servants in all assaults of our enemies; that we, surely trusting in thy defence, may not fear the power of any adversaries, through the might of Jesus Christ our Lord. *Amen.*

*The third Collect, for Grace.*
O  L O R D , our heavenly Father, Almighty and everlasting God, who hast safely brought us to the beginning of this day; Defend us in the same with thy mighty power; and grant that this day we fall into no sin, neither run into any kind of danger; but that all our doings may be ordered by thy governance, to do always that is righteous in thy sight; through Jesus Christ our Lord. *Amen.*

¶ *In Quires and Places where they sing, here followeth the Anthem.*

# THE LITANY

¶ *Here followeth the LITANY, or General Supplication, to be sung or said after Morning Prayer upon* Sundays, Wednesdays, *and* Fridays, *and at other times when it shall be commanded by the Ordinary.*

O G O D the Father, of heaven: have mercy upon us miserable sinners.

*O God the Father, of heaven: have mercy upon us miserable sinners.*

O God the Son, Redeemer of the world: have mercy upon us miserable sinners.

*O God the Son, Redeemer of the world: have mercy upon us miserable sinners.*

O God the Holy Ghost, proceeding from the Father and the Son: have mercy upon us miserable sinners.

*O God the Holy Ghost, proceeding from the Father and the Son: have mercy upon us miserable sinners.*

O holy, blessed, and glorious Trinity, three Persons and one God: have mercy upon us miserable sinners.

*O holy, blessed, and glorious Trinity, three Persons and one God: have mercy upon us miserable sinners.*

Remember not, Lord, our offences, nor the offences of our forefathers; neither take thou vengeance of our sins: spare us, good Lord, spare thy people, whom thou hast redeemed with thy most precious blood, and be not angry with us for ever.

*Spare us, good Lord.*

From all evil and mischief; from sin, from the crafts and assaults of the devil; from thy wrath, and from everlasting damnation,

*Good Lord, deliver us.*

From all blindness of heart; from pride, vain-glory, and hypocrisy; from envy, hatred, and malice, and all uncharitableness,

*Good Lord, deliver us.*

From fornication, and all other deadly sin; and from all the deceits of the world, the flesh, and the devil,

*Good Lord, deliver us.*

From lightning and tempest; from plague, pestilence, and famine; from battle and murder, and from sudden death,

*Good Lord, deliver us.*

From all sedition, privy conspiracy, and rebellion; from all false doctrine, heresy, and schism; from hardness of heart, and contempt of thy Word and Commandment,

*Good Lord, deliver us.*

By the mystery of thy holy Incarnation; by thy holy Nativity and Circumcision; by thy Baptism, Fasting, and Temptation,

*Good Lord, deliver us.*

By thine Agony and bloody Sweat; by thy Cross and Passion; by thy precious Death and Burial; by thy glorious Resurrection and Ascension; and

by the coming of the Holy Ghost,
*Good Lord, deliver us.*

In all time of our tribulation; in all time of our wealth; in the hour of death, and in the day of judgement,
*Good Lord, deliver us.*

We sinners do beseech thee to hear us, O Lord God; and that it may please thee to rule and govern thy holy Church universal in the right way;
*We beseech thee to hear us, good Lord.*

That it may please thee to keep and strengthen in the true worshipping of thee, in righteousness and holiness of life, thy Servant George, our most gracious King and Governour;
*We beseech thee to hear us, good Lord.*

That it may please thee to rule his heart in thy faith, fear, and love, and that he may evermore have affiance in thee, and ever seek thy honour and glory;
*We beseech thee to hear us, good Lord.*

That it may please thee to be his defender and keeper, giving him the victory over all his enemies;
*We beseech thee to hear us, good Lord.*

That it may please thee to bless and preserve our gracious Queen Charlotte, their royal highnesses, George Prince of Wales, the Dowager Princess of Wales and all the Royal Family;
*We beseech thee to hear us, good Lord.*

That it may please thee to illuminate all Bishops, Priests, and Deacons, with true knowledge and understanding of thy Word; and that both by their preaching and living they may set it forth, and shew it accordingly;

*We beseech thee to hear us, good Lord.*

That it may please thee to endue the Lords of the Council, and all the Nobility, with grace, wisdom, and understanding;
*We beseech thee to hear us, good Lord.*

That it may please thee to bless and keep the Magistrates, giving them grace to execute justice, and to maintain truth;
*We beseech thee to hear us, good Lord.*

That it may please thee to bless and keep all thy people;
*We beseech thee to hear us, good Lord.*

That it may please thee to give to all nations unity, peace, and concord;
*We beseech thee to hear us, good Lord.*

That it may please thee to give us an heart to love and dread thee, and diligently to live after thy commandments;
*We beseech thee to hear us, good Lord.*

That it may please thee to give to all thy people increase of grace to hear meekly thy Word, and to receive it with pure affection, and to bring forth the fruits of the Spirit;
*We beseech thee to hear us, good Lord.*

That it may please thee to bring into the way of truth all such as have erred, and are deceived;
*We beseech thee to hear us, good Lord.*

That it may please thee to strengthen such as do stand; and to comfort and help the weak-hearted; and to raise up them that fall; and finally to beat down Satan under our feet;

*We beseech thee to hear us, good Lord.*

That it may please thee to succour, help, and comfort, all that are in danger, necessity, and tribulation;

*We beseech thee to hear us, good Lord.*

That it may please thee to preserve all that travel by land or by water, all women labouring of child, all sick persons, and young children; and to shew thy pity upon all prisoners and captives;

*We beseech thee to hear us, good Lord.*

That it may please thee to defend, and provide for, the fatherless children, and widows, and all that are desolate and oppressed;

*We beseech thee to hear us, good Lord.*

That it may please thee to have mercy upon all men;

*We beseech thee to hear us, good Lord.*

That it may please thee to forgive our enemies, persecutors, and slanderers, and to turn their hearts;

*We beseech thee to hear us, good Lord.*

That it may please thee to give and preserve to our use the kindly fruits of the earth, so as in due time we may enjoy them;

*We beseech thee to hear us, good Lord.*

That it may please thee to give us true repentance; to forgive us all our sins, negligences, and ignorances; and to endue us with the grace of thy Holy Spirit to amend our lives according to thy holy Word;

*We beseech thee to hear us, good Lord.*

Son of God: we beseech thee to hear us.

*Son of God: we beseech thee to hear us.*

O Lamb of God: that takest away the sins of the world;

*Grant us thy peace.*

O Lamb of God: that takest away the sins of the world;

*Have mercy upon us.*

O Christ, hear us.

*O Christ, hear us.*

Lord, have mercy upon us.

*Lord, have mercy upon us.*

Christ, have mercy upon us.

*Christ, have mercy upon us.*

Lord, have mercy upon us.

*Lord, have mercy upon us.*

¶ *Then shall the Priest, and the people with him, say the Lord's Prayer.*

O U R Father, which art in heaven, Hallowed be thy Name. Thy kingdom come. Thy will be done in earth, As it is in heaven. Give us this day our daily bread. And forgive us our trespasses, As we forgive them that trespass against us. And lead us not into temptation; But deliver us from evil. Amen.

PRIEST. O Lord, deal not with us after our sins.

ANSWER. Neither reward us after our iniquities.

Let us pray.

O G O D, merciful Father, that despisest not the sighing of a contrite heart, nor the desire of such as be sorrowful; Mercifully assist our prayers that we make before thee in all our troubles and adversities, whensoever they oppress us; and graciously hear us, that those evils, which the craft and subtilty of the devil or man worketh against us, be brought to nought; and by the providence of thy goodness they may be dispersed; that we thy servants, being hurt by no persecutions, may evermore give thanks unto thee in thy holy Church; through Jesus Christ our Lord.

*O Lord, arise, help us, and deliver us for thy Name's sake.*

O GOD, we have heard with our ears, and our fathers have declared unto us, the noble works that thou didst in their days; and in the old time before them.

*O Lord, arise, help us, and deliver us for thine honour.*

Glory be to the Father, and to the Son: and to the Holy Ghost;

ANSWER. As it was in the beginning, is now, and ever shall be: world without end. Amen.

From our enemies defend us, O Christ.

*Graciously look upon our afflictions.*

Pitifully behold the sorrows of our hearts.

*Mercifully forgive the sins of thy people.*

Favourably with mercy hear our prayers.

*O Son of David, have mercy upon us.*

Both now and ever vouchsafe to hear us, O Christ.

*Graciously hear us, O Christ; graciously hear us, O Lord Christ.*

PRIEST. O Lord, let thy mercy be shewed upon us;

ANSWER. As we do put our trust in thee.

Let us pray.

WE HUMBLY beseech thee, O Father, mercifully to look upon our infirmities; and for the glory of thy Name turn from us all those evils that we most righteously have deserved; and grant, that in all our troubles we may put our whole trust and confidence in thy mercy, and evermore serve thee in holiness and pureness of living, to thy honour and glory; through our only Mediator and Advocate, Jesus Christ our Lord. *Amen.*

*A Prayer of* St. Chrysostom.

ALMIGHTY God, who hast given us grace at this time with one accord to make our common supplications unto thee; and dost promise, that when two or three are gathered together in thy Name thou wilt grant their requests; Fulfil now, O Lord, the desires and petitions of thy servants, as may be most expedient for them; granting us in this world knowledge of thy truth, and in the world to come life everlasting. *Amen.*

2 *Cor.* xiii.

THE grace of our Lord Jesus Christ, and the love of God, and the fellowship of the Holy Ghost, be with us all evermore. *Amen.*

*Here endeth the LITANY.*

# The order of the
## ADMINISTRATION OF THE LORD'S SUPPER
## *or HOLY COMMUNION*

¶ *SO many as intend to be partakers of the holy Communion shall signify their names to the Curate, at least some time the day before.*

¶ *And if any of those be an open and notorious evil liver, or have done any wrong to his neighbours by word or deed, so that the Congregation be thereby offended; the Curate, having knowledge thereof, shall call him and advertise him, that in any wise he presume not to come to the Lord's Table, until he hath openly declared himself to have truly repented and amended his former naughty life, that the Congregation may thereby be satisfied, which before were offended; and that he hath recompensed the parties, to whom he hath done wrong; or at least declare himself to be in full purpose so to do, as soon as he conveniently may.*

¶ *The same order shall the Curate use with those betwixt whom he perceiveth malice and hatred to reign; not suffering them to be partakers of the Lord's Table, until he know them to be reconciled. And if one of the parties so at variance be content to forgive from the bottom of his heart all that the other hath trespassed against him, and to make amends for that he himself hath offended; and the other party will not be persuaded to a godly unity, but remain still in his frowardness and malice: the Minister in that case ought to admit the penitent person to the holy Communion, and not him that is obstinate. Provided that every Minister so repelling any, as is specified in this, or the next precedent Paragraph of this Rubrick, shall be obliged to give an account of the same to the Ordinary within fourteen days after at the farthest. And the Ordinary shall proceed against the offending person according to the Canon.*

¶ *The Table, at the Communion-time having a fair white linen cloth upon it, shall stand in the Body of the Church, or in the Chancel, where Morning and Evening Prayer are appointed to be said. And the Priest standing at the North-side of the Table shall say the Lord's Prayer, with the Collect following, the people kneeling.*

OUR Father, which art in heaven, Hallowed be thy Name. Thy kingdom come. Thy will be done in earth, As it is in heaven. Give us this day our daily bread. And forgive us our trespasses, As we forgive them that trespass against us. And lead us not into temptation; But deliver us from evil. Amen.

*The Collect.*

ALMIGHTY God, unto whom all hearts be open, all desires known, and from whom no secrets are hid; Cleanse the thoughts of our hearts by the inspiration of thy Holy Spirit, that we may perfectly love thee, and worthily magnify thy holy Name; through Christ our Lord. *Amen.*

¶ *Then shall the Priest, turning to the people, rehearse distinctly all the TEN COMMANDMENTS; and the people still kneeling shall, after every Commandment, ask God mercy for their transgression thereof for the time past, and grace to keep the same for the time to come, as followeth.*

MINISTER.

GOD spake these words, and said; I am the Lord thy God: Thou shalt have none other gods but me.

PEOPLE. Lord, have mercy upon us, and incline our hearts to keep this law.

MINISTER. Thou shalt not make to thyself any graven image, nor the likeness of any thing that is in heaven above, or in the earth beneath, or in the water under the earth. Thou shalt not bow down to them, nor worship them: for I the Lord thy God am a jealous God, and visit the sins of the fathers upon the children, unto the third and fourth generation of them that hate me, and shew mercy unto thousands in them that love me, and keep my commandments.

PEOPLE. Lord, have mercy upon us, and incline our hearts to keep this law.

MINISTER. Thou shalt not take the Name of the Lord thy God in vain: for the Lord will not hold him guiltless, that taketh his Name in vain.

PEOPLE. Lord, have mercy upon us, and incline our hearts to keep this law.

MINISTER. Remember that thou keep holy the Sabbath-day. Six days shalt thou labour, and do all that thou hast to do; but the seventh day is the Sabbath of the Lord thy God. In it thou shalt do no manner of work, thou, and thy son, and thy daughter, thy man-servant, and thy maid-servant, thy cattle, and the stranger that is within thy gates. For in six days the Lord made heaven and earth, the sea, and all that in them is, and rested the seventh day: wherefore the Lord blessed the seventh day, and hallowed it.

PEOPLE. Lord, have mercy upon us, and incline our hearts to keep this law.

MINISTER. Honour thy father and thy mother; that thy days may be long in the land, which the Lord thy God giveth thee.

PEOPLE. Lord, have mercy upon us, and incline our hearts to keep this law.

MINISTER. Thou shalt do no murder.

PEOPLE. Lord, have mercy upon us, and incline our hearts to keep this law.

MINISTER. Thou shalt not commit adultery.

PEOPLE. Lord, have mercy upon us, and incline our hearts to keep this law.

MINISTER. Thou shalt not steal.

PEOPLE. Lord, have mercy upon us, and incline our hearts to keep this law.

MINISTER. Thou shalt not bear false witness against thy neighbour.

PEOPLE. Lord, have mercy upon us, and incline our hearts to keep this law.

MINISTER. Thou shalt not covet thy neighbour's house, thou shalt not covet thy neighbour's wife, nor his servant, nor his maid, nor his ox, nor his ass, nor any thing that is his.

PEOPLE. Lord, have mercy upon us, and write all these thy laws in our hearts, we beseech thee.

¶ *Then shall follow one of these two Collects for the King, the Priest standing as before, and saying,*

Let us pray.

ALMIGHTY God, whose kingdom is everlasting, and power infinite; Have mercy upon the whole Church; and so rule the heart of thy chosen servant George, our King and Governour, that he (knowing whose minister he is) may above all things seek thy honour and glory: and that we, and all his subjects (duly considering whose authority he hath) may faithfully serve, honour, and humbly obey him, in thee, and for thee, according to thy blessed Word and ordinance; through Jesus Christ our Lord, who with thee and the Holy Ghost liveth and reigneth, ever one God, world without end. *Amen.*

*Or,*

ALMIGHTY and everlasting God, we are taught by thy holy Word, that the hearts of Kings are in thy rule and governance, and that thou dost dispose and turn them as it seemeth best to thy godly wisdom: We humbly beseech thee so to dispose and govern the heart of George thy Servant, our King and Governour, that, in all his thoughts, words, and works, he may ever seek thy honour and glory, and study to preserve thy people committed to his charge, in wealth, peace, and godliness: Grant this, O merciful Father, for thy dear Son's sake, Jesus Christ our Lord. *Amen.*

¶ *Then shall be said the Collect of the Day. And immediately after the Collect the Priest shall read the Epistle, saying,* The Epistle [*or,* The portion of Scripture appointed for the Epistle] is written in the —— Chapter of —— beginning at the —— Verse. *And the Epistle ended, he shall say,* Here endeth the Epistle. *Then shall he read the Gospel (the people all standing up) saying,* The holy Gospel is written in the —— Chapter of —— beginning at the —— Verse. *And the Gospel ended, shall be sung or said the Creed following, the people still standing, as before.*

I BELIEVE in one God the Father Almighty, Maker of heaven and earth, And of all things visible and invisible:

And in one Lord Jesus Christ, the only-begotten Son of God, Begotten of his Father before all worlds, God of God, Light of Light, Very God of very God, Begotten, not made, Being of one substance with the Father; By whom all things were made, Who for us men, and for our salvation came down from heaven, And was incarnate by the Holy Ghost of the Virgin Mary, And was made man, And was crucified also for us under Pontius Pilate. He suffered and was buried, And the third day he rose again according to the Scriptures, And ascended into heaven, And sitteth on the right hand of the Father. And he shall come again with glory to judge both the quick and the dead: Whose kingdom shall have no end.

And I believe in the Holy Ghost, The Lord and Giver of life, Who proceedeth from the Father and the Son, Who with the Father and the Son together is worshipped and glorified, Who spake by the Prophets. And I believe one Catholick and Apostolick Church. I acknowledge one Baptism for the remission of sins, And I look for the Resurrection of the dead, And the life of the world to come. Amen.

¶ *Then the Curate shall declare unto the people what Holy-days, or Fasting-days, are in the Week following to be observed. And then also (if occasion be) shall notice be given of the Communion; and Briefs, Citations, and Excommunications read. And nothing shall be proclaimed or published in the Church, during the time of Divine Service, but by the Minister: nor by him any thing, but what is prescribed in the Rules of this Book, or enjoined by the King or by the Ordinary of the place.*

¶ *Then shall follow the Sermon, or one of the Homilies already set forth, or hereafter to be set forth, by authority.*

¶ *Then shall the Priest return to the Lord's Table, and begin the Offertory, saying one or more of these Sentences following, as he thinketh most convenient in his discretion.*

L E T your light so shine before men, that they may see your good works, and glorify your Father which is in heaven.        *St. Matth.* v.

Lay not up for yourselves treasure upon the earth; where the rust and moth doth corrupt, and where thieves break through and steal: but lay up for yourselves treasures in heaven; where neither rust nor moth doth corrupt, and where thieves do not break through and steal.        *St. Matth.* vi.

Whatsoever ye would that men should do unto you, even so do unto them; for this is the Law and the Prophets.        *St. Matth.* vii.

Not every one that saith unto me, Lord, Lord, shall enter into the Kingdom of heaven; but he that doeth the will of my Father which is in heaven.
        *St. Matth.* vii.

Zacchæus stood forth, and said unto the Lord, Behold, Lord, the half of my goods I give to the poor; and if I have done any wrong to any man, I restore four-fold.        *St. Luke* xix.

Who goeth a warfare at any time of his own cost? Who planteth a vineyard, and eateth not of the fruit thereof? Or who feedeth a flock, and eateth not of the milk of the flock?
        1 *Cor.* ix.

If we have sown unto you spiritual things, is it a great matter if we shall reap your worldly things? 1 *Cor.* ix.

Do ye not know, that they who minister about holy things live of the sacrifice; and they who wait at the altar are partakers with the altar? Even so hath the Lord also ordained, that they who preach the Gospel should live of the Gospel.        1 *Cor.* ix.

He that soweth little shall reap little; and he that soweth plenteously shall reap plenteously. Let every man do according as he is disposed in his heart, not grudgingly, or of necessity; for God loveth a cheerful giver.
        2 *Cor.* ix.

Let him that is taught in the Word

minister unto him that teacheth, in all good things. Be not deceived, God is not mocked: for whatsoever a man soweth that shall he reap.   *Gal*. vi.

While we have time, let us do good unto all men; and specially unto them that are of the household of faith.
*Gal*. vi.

Godliness is great riches, if a man be content with that he hath: for we brought nothing into the world, neither may we carry any thing out.
1 *Tim*. vi.

Charge them who are rich in this world, that they be ready to give, and glad to distribute; laying up in store for themselves a good foundation against the time to come, that they may attain eternal life.   1 *Tim*. vi.

God is not unrighteous, that he will forget your works, and labour that proceedeth of love; which love ye have shewed for his Name's sake, who have ministered unto the saints, and yet do minister.   *Heb*. vi.

To do good, and to distribute, forget not; for with such sacrifices God is well pleased.   *Heb*. xiii.

Whoso hath this world's good, and seeth his brother have need, and shutteth up his compassion from him, how dwelleth the love of God in him?
1 *St. John* iii.

Give alms of thy goods, and never turn thy face from any poor man; and then the face of the Lord shall not be turned away from thee.   *Tob*. iv.

Be merciful after thy power. If thou hast much, give plenteously: if thou hast little, do thy diligence gladly to give of that little: for so gatherest thou thyself a good reward in the day of necessity.   *Tob*. iv.

He that hath pity upon the poor lendeth unto the Lord: and look, what he layeth out, it shall be paid him again.   *Prov*. xix.

Blessed be the man that provideth for the sick and needy: the Lord shall deliver him in the time of trouble.
*Psal*. xli.

¶ *Whilst these Sentences are in reading, the Deacons, Church-wardens, or other fit person appointed for that purpose, shall receive the Alms for the poor, and other devotions of the people, in a decent bason to be provided by the Parish for that purpose; and reverently bring it to the Priest, who shall humbly present and place it upon the holy Table.*

¶ *And when there is a Communion, the Priest shall then place upon the Table so much Bread and Wine, as he shall think sufficient.*
*After which done, the Priest shall say,*

Let us pray for the whole state of Christ's Church militant here in earth.

ALMIGHTY and everliving God, who by thy holy Apostle hast taught us to make prayers, and supplications, and to give thanks, for all men; We humbly beseech thee most mercifully [*to accept our alms and oblations, and*] to receive these our prayers, which we offer unto thy Divine Majesty; beseeching thee to inspire continually the universal Church with the spirit of truth, unity, and concord: And grant, that all they that do confess thy holy Name may agree in the truth of thy holy Word, and live in unity, and godly love. We beseech thee also to save and defend all Christian Kings, Princes, and Governours; and specially thy servant George our King; that under him we may be godly and quietly governed: And grant unto his whole Council, and to all that are put in authority under him, that they may truly and indifferently minister justice, to the punishment of wickedness and vice, and to the maintenance of thy true religion, and virtue. Give grace, O heavenly Father, to all Bishops and Curates, that they may both by their life and doctrine set forth thy true and lively Word, and rightly and duly administer thy holy Sacraments: And to all thy people give thy heavenly grace; and especially to this congregation here present; that, with meet heart and due reverence, they may hear, and receive thy holy Word; truly serving thee in holiness and righteousness all the days of their life. And we most humbly beseech thee of thy goodness, O Lord, to comfort and succour all them, who in this transitory life are in trouble, sorrow, need, sickness, or any other adversity. And we also bless thy holy Name for all thy servants departed this life in thy faith and fear; beseeching thee to give us grace so to follow their good examples, that with them we may be partakers of thy heavenly kingdom: Grant this, O Father, for Jesus Christ's sake, our only Mediator and Advocate. *Amen.*

¶ *In case the Minister shall see the people negligent to come to the holy Communion, he shall use this Exhortation.*

DEARLY beloved brethren, on — — I intend, by God's grace, to celebrate the Lord's Supper: unto which, in God's behalf, I bid you all that are here present; and beseech you, for the Lord Jesus Christ's sake, that ye will not refuse to come thereto, being so lovingly called and bidden by God himself. Ye know how grievous and unkind a thing it is, when a man hath prepared a rich feast, decked his table with all kind of provision, so that there lacketh nothing but the guests to sit down; and yet they who are called (without any cause) most unthankfully refuse to come. Which of you in such a case would not be moved? Who would not think a great injury and wrong done unto him? Wherefore, most dearly beloved in Christ, take ye good heed, lest ye, withdrawing yourselves from this holy Supper, provoke God's indignation against you. It is an easy matter for a man to say, I will not communicate, because I am otherwise hindered with worldly business. But such excuses are not so easily accepted and allowed before God. If any man say, I am a grievous sinner, and therefore am afraid to come: wherefore then do ye not repent and amend? When God calleth you, are ye not ashamed to say ye will not come? When ye should return to God, will ye excuse yourselves, and say ye are not ready? Consider earnestly with yourselves how little such feigned excuses will avail before God. They that refused the feast in the Gospel, because they had bought a farm, or would try their yokes of oxen, or because they were married, were not so excused, but counted unworthy of the heavenly feast. I, for my part, shall be ready; and, according to mine Office, I bid you in the Name of God, I call you in Christ's behalf, I exhort you, as ye love your own salvation, that ye will be partakers of this holy Communion. And as the Son of God did vouchsafe to yield up his soul by death upon the Cross for your salvation; so it is your duty to receive the Communion in remembrance of the sacrifice of his death, as he himself hath commanded: which if ye shall neglect to do, consider with yourselves how great injury ye do unto God, and how sore punishment hangeth over your heads for the same; when ye wilfully abstain from the Lord's Table, and separate from your brethren, who come to feed on the banquet of that most heavenly food. These things if ye earnestly consider, ye will be God's grace return to a better mind: for the obtaining whereof we shall not cease to make our humble petitions unto Almighty God our heavenly Father.

¶ *At the time of the celebration of the Communion, the Communicants being conveniently placed for the receiving of the holy Sacrament, the Priest shall say this Exhortation.*

D E A R L Y beloved in the Lord, ye that mind to come to the holy Communion of the Body and Blood of our Saviour Christ, must consider how Saint Paul exhorteth all persons diligently to try and examine themselves, before they presume to eat of that Bread, and drink of that Cup. For as the benefit is great, if with a true penitent heart and lively faith we receive that holy Sacrament; (for then we spiritually eat the flesh of Christ, and drink his blood; then we dwell in Christ, and Christ in us; we are one with Christ, and Christ with us;) so is the danger great, if we receive the same unworthily. For then we are guilty of the Body and Blood of Christ our Saviour; we eat and drink our own damna-

tion, not considering the Lord's Body; we kindle God's wrath against us; we provoke him to plague us with divers diseases, and sundry kinds of death. Judge therefore yourselves, brethren, that ye be not judged of the Lord; repent you truly for your sins past; have a lively and stedfast faith in Christ our Saviour; amend your lives, and be in perfect charity with all men; so shall ye be meet partakers of those holy mysteries. And above all things ye must give most humble and hearty thanks to God, the Father, the Son, and the Holy Ghost, for the redemption of the world by the death and passion of our Saviour Christ, both God and man; who did humble himself, even to the death upon the Cross, for us, miserable sinners, who lay in darkness and the shadow of death; that he might make us the children of God, and exalt us to everlasting life. And to the end that we should alway remember the exceeding great love of our Master, and only Saviour, Jesus Christ, thus dying for us, and the innumerable benefits which by his precious blood-shedding he hath obtained to us; he hath instituted and ordained holy mysteries, as pledges of his love, and for a continual remembrance of his death, to our great and endless comfort. To him therefore, with the Father and the Holy Ghost, let us give (as we are most bounden) continual thanks; submitting ourselves wholly to his holy will and pleasure, and studying to serve him in true holiness and righteousness all the days of our life. *Amen.*

¶ *Then shall the Priest say to them that come to receive the holy Communion,*

YE THAT do truly and earnestly repent you of your sins, and are in love and charity with your neighbours, and intend to lead a new life, following the commandments of God, and walking from henceforth in his holy ways; Draw near with faith, and take this holy Sacrament to your comfort; and make your humble confession to Almighty God, meekly kneeling upon your knees.

¶ *Then shall this general Confession be made, in the name of all those that are minded to receive the holy Communion, by one of the Ministers; both he and all the people kneeling humbly upon their knees, and saying,*

ALMIGHTY God, Father of our Lord Jesus Christ, Maker of all things, Judge of all men; We acknowledge and bewail our manifold sins and wickedness, Which we, from time to time, most grievously have committed, By thought, word, and deed, Against thy Divine Majesty, Provoking most justly thy wrath and indignation against us. We do earnestly repent, And are heartily sorry for these our misdoings; The remembrance of them is grievous unto us; The burden of them is intolerable. Have mercy upon us, Have mercy upon us, most merciful Father; For thy Son our Lord Jesus Christ's sake, Forgive us all that is past; And grant that we may ever hereafter Serve and please thee In newness of life, To the honour and glory of thy Name; Through Jesus Christ our Lord. Amen.

¶ *Then shall the Priest (or the Bishop, being present,) stand up, and turning himself to the people, pronounce this Absolution.*

ALMIGHTY God, our heavenly Father, who of his great mercy hath promised forgiveness of sins to all them that with hearty repentance and true faith turn unto him; Have mercy upon you; pardon and deliver you from all your sins; confirm and strengthen you in all goodness; and bring you to everlasting life; through Jesus Christ our Lord. *Amen.*

¶ *Then shall the Priest say,*

Hear what comfortable words our Saviour Christ saith unto all that truly turn to him.
COME unto me all that travail and are heavy laden, and I will refresh you.        *St. Matth.* xi. 28.
So God loved the world, that he gave his only-begotten Son, to the end that all that believe in him should not perish, but have everlasting life.
                    *St. John* iii. 16.
Hear also what Saint Paul saith.
This is a true saying, and worthy of all men to be received, That Christ Jesus came into the world to save sinners.        1 *Tim.* i. 15.
Hear also what Saint John saith.
If any man sin, we have an Advocate with the Father, Jesus Christ the righteous; and he is the propitiation for our sins.        1 *St. John* ii. 1.

¶ *After which the Priest shall proceed, saying,*

Lift up your hearts.
ANSWER. We lift them up unto the Lord.
PRIEST. Let us give thanks unto our Lord God.
ANSWER. It is meet and right so to do.

¶ *Then shall the Priest turn to the Lord's Table, and say,*

IT IS very meet, right, and our bounden duty, that we should at all times, and in all places, give thanks unto thee, O Lord, Holy Father, Almighty, Everlasting God.

¶ *These words* [Holy Father] *must be omitted on* Trinity-Sunday.

¶ *Here shall follow the Proper Preface, according to the time, if there be any specially appointed: or else immediately shall follow,*

THEREFORE with Angels and Archangels, and with all the company of heaven, we laud and magnify thy glorious Name; evermore praising thee, and saying, Holy, holy, holy, Lord God of hosts, heaven and earth are fully of thy glory: Glory be to thee, O Lord most High. *Amen.*

*Proper Prefaces.*
*Upon* Christmas-day, *and seven days after.*
BECAUSE thou didst give Jesus Christ thine only Son to be born as at this time for us; who, by the operation of the Holy Ghost, was made very man of the substance of the Virgin Mary his mother; and that without spot of sin, to make us clean from all sin. Therefore with Angels, &c.

*Upon* Easter-day, *and seven days after.*
BUT chiefly are we bound to praise thee for the glorious Resurrection of thy Son Jesus Christ our Lord: for he is the very Paschal Lamb, which was offered for us, and hath taken away the sin of the world; who by his death hath destroyed death, and by his rising to life again hath restored to us everlasting life. Therefore with Angels, &c.

*Upon* Ascension-day, *and seven days after.*

THROUGH thy most dearly beloved Son Jesus Christ our Lord; who after his most glorious Resurrection manifestly appeared to all his Apostles, and in their sight ascended up into heaven to prepare a place for us; that where he is, thither we might also ascend, and reign with him in glory. Therefore with Angels, &c.

*Upon* Whit-sunday, *and six days after.*
THROUGH Jesus Christ our Lord; according to whose most true promise, the Holy Ghost came down as at this time from heaven with a sudden great sound, as it had been a mighty wind, in the likeness of fiery tongues, lighting upon the Apostles, to teach them, and to lead them to all truth; giving them both the gift of divers languages, and also boldness with fervent zeal constantly to preach the Gospel unto all nations; whereby we have been brought out of darkness and error into the clear light and true knowledge of thee, and of thy Son Jesus Christ. Therefore with Angels, &c.

*Upon the Feast of* Trinity *only.*
WHO art one God, one Lord; not one only Person, but three Persons in one Substance. For that which we believe of the glory of the Father, the same we believe of the Son, and of the Holy Ghost, without any difference or inequality. Therefore with Angels, &c.

¶ *After each of which Prefaces shall immediately be sung or said,*

THEREFORE with Angels and Archangels, and with all the company of heaven, we laud and magnify thy glorious Name; evermore praising thee, and saying, Holy, holy, holy,

Lord God of hosts, heaven and earth are full of thy glory: Glory be to thee, O Lord most High. *Amen.*

¶ *Then shall the Priest, kneeling down at the Lord's Table, say in the name of all them that shall receive the Communion this Prayer following.*

W E  D O not presume to come to this thy Table, O merciful Lord, trusting in our own righteousness, but in thy manifold and great mercies. We are not worthy so much as to gather up the crumbs under thy Table. But thou art the same Lord, whose property is always to have mercy: Grant us therefore, gracious Lord, so to eat the flesh of thy dear Son Jesus Christ, and to drink his blood, that our sinful bodies may be made clean by his body, and our souls washed through his most precious blood, and that we may evermore dwell in him, and he in us. *Amen.*

¶ *When the Priest, standing before the Table, hath so ordered the Bread and Wine, that he may with the more readiness and decency break the Bread before the people, and take the Cup into his hands, he shall say the Prayer of Consecration, as followeth.*

A L M I G H T Y God, our heavenly Father, who of thy tender mercy didst give thine only Son Jesus Christ to suffer death upon the cross for our redemption; who made there (by his one oblation of himself once offered) a full, perfect, and sufficient sacrifice, oblation, and satisfaction, for the sins of the whole world; and did institute, and in his holy Gospel command us to continue, a perpetual memory of that his precious death, until his coming again; Hear us, O merciful Father, we most humbly beseech thee; and grant that we receiving these thy creatures of bread and wine, according to thy Son our Saviour Jesus Christ's holy institution, in remembrance of his death and passion, may be partakers of his most blessed Body and Blood: who, in the same night that he was betrayed,

*took    Bread;    *Here the Priest and, when he had *is to take the Paten* given thanks, †he *into his hands:* brake it, and gave it to his dis- †And  here  to ciples,  saying, *break the Bread:* Take, eat, *this is my body which *And here to lay is given for you: *his hand upon all* Do this in remem- *the Bread.* brance of me. Likewise after supper he †took †Here  he  is  to the Cup; and, *take the Cup into* when he had *his hand:* given   thanks, he gave it to them, saying, Drink ye all of this; for this *is my Blood *And here to lay of the New Tes- *his   hand   upon* tament, which is *every vessel (be it* shed for you and *Chalice or Flagon)* for many for the *in  which  there  is* remission of sins: *any  Wine  to  be* *consecrated.* Do this, as oft as ye shall drink it, in remembrance of me. *Amen.*

¶ *Then shall the Minister first receive the Communion in both kinds himself, and then proceed to deliver the same to the Bishops, Priests, and Deacons, in like manner, (if any be present,) and after that to the people also in order, into their hands, all meekly kneeling. And, when he delivereth the Bread to any one, he shall say,*

THE Body of our Lord Jesus Christ, which was given for thee, preserve thy body and soul unto everlasting life. Take and eat this in remembrance that Christ died for thee, and feed on him in thy heart by faith with thanksgiving.

¶ *And the Minister that delivereth the Cup to any one shall say,*

THE Blood of our Lord Jesus Christ, which was shed for thee, preserve thy body and soul unto everlasting life. Drink this in remembrance that Christ's Blood was shed for thee, and be thankful.

¶ *If the consecrated Bread or Wine be all spent before all have communicated, the Priest is to consecrate more according to the Form before prescribed; beginning at* [Our Saviour Christ in the same night, &c.] *for the blessing of the Bread; and at* [Likewise after Supper, &c.] *for the blessing of the Cup.*

¶ *When all have communicated, the Minister shall return to the Lord's Table, and reverently place upon it what remaineth of the consecrated Elements, covering the same with a fair linen cloth.*

¶ *Then shall the Priest say the Lord's Prayer, the people repeating after him every Petition.*

OUR Father, which art in heaven, Hallowed be thy Name. Thy kingdom come. Thy will be done in earth, As it is in heaven. Give us this day our daily bread. And forgive us our trespasses, As we forgive them that trespass against us. And lead us not into temptation; But deliver us from evil: For thine is the kingdom; The power, and the glory, For ever and ever. Amen.

¶ *After shall be said as followeth.*

O LORD and heavenly Father, we thy humble servants entirely desire thy fatherly goodness mercifully to accept this our sacrifice of praise and thanksgiving; most humbly beseeching thee to grant, that by the merits and death of thy Son Jesus Christ, and through faith in his blood, we and all thy whole Church may obtain remission of our sins, and all other benefits of his passion. And here we offer and present unto thee, O Lord, ourselves, our souls and bodies, to be a reasonable, holy, and lively sacrifice unto thee; humbly beseeching thee, that all we, who are partakers of this holy Communion, may be fulfilled with thy grace and heavenly benediction. And although we be unworthy, through our manifold sins, to offer unto thee any sacrifice, yet we beseech thee to accept this our bounden duty and service; not weighing our merits, but pardoning our offences, through Jesus Christ our Lord; by whom, and with whom, in the unity of the Holy Ghost, all honour and glory be unto thee, O Father Almighty, world without end. *Amen.*

*Or this.*

ALMIGHTY and everliving God, we most heartily thank thee, for that thou dost vouchsafe to feed us, who have duly received these holy mysteries, with the spiritual food of the most precious Body and Blood of thy Son our Saviour Jesus Christ; and dost assure us thereby of thy favour and goodness towards us; and that we are very members incorporate in the mystical body of thy Son, which is the blessed company of all faithful people; and are also heirs through hope of thy everlasting kingdom, by the merits of the most precious death and passion of thy dear Son. And we most humbly beseech thee, O heavenly Father, so to assist us with thy grace, that we may continue in that holy fellowship, and do all such good works as thou hast prepared for us to walk in; through Jesus Christ our Lord, to whom, with thee and the Holy Ghost, be all honour and glory, world without end. *Amen.*

¶ *Then shall be said or sung,*

GLORY be to God on high, and in earth peace, good will towards men. We praise thee, we bless thee, we worship thee, we glorify thee, we give thanks to thee for thy great glory, O Lord God, heavenly King, God the Father Almighty.

O Lord, the only-begotten Son Jesu Christ; O Lord God, Lamb of God, Son of the Father, that takest away the sins of the world, have mercy upon us. Thou that takest away the sins of the world, have mercy upon us. Thou that takest away the sins of the world, receive our prayer. Thou that sittest at the right hand of God the Father, have mercy upon us.

For thou only art holy; thou only art the Lord; thou only, O Christ, with the Holy Ghost, art most high in the glory of God the Father. *Amen.*

¶ *Then the Priest (or Bishop if he be present) shall let them depart with this Blessing.*

THE peace of God, which passeth all understanding, keep your hearts and minds in the knowledge and love of God, and of his Son Jesus Christ our Lord: and the blessing of God Almighty, the Father, the Son, and the Holy Ghost, be amongst you and remain with you always. *Amen.*

¶ *Collects to be said after the Offertory, when there is no Communion, every such day one or more; and the same may be said also, as often as occasion shall serve, after the Collects either of Morning or Evening Prayer, Communion, or Litany, by the discretion of the Minister.*

ASSIST us mercifully, O Lord, in these our supplications and prayers, and dispose the way of thy servants towards the attainment of everlasting salvation; that, among all the changes and chances of this mortal life, they may ever be defended by thy most gracious and ready help; through Jesus Christ our Lord. *Amen.*

O ALMIGHTY Lord, and everlasting God, vouchsafe, we beseech thee, to direct, sanctify, and govern, both our hearts and bodies, in the ways of thy laws, and in the works of thy commandments; that through thy most mighty protection, both here and ever, we may be preserved in body and soul; through our Lord and Saviour Jesus Christ. *Amen.*

GRANT, we beseech thee, Almighty God, that the words, which we have heard this day with our outward ears, may through thy grace be so grafted inwardly in our hearts, that they may bring forth in us the fruit of good living, to the honour and praise of thy Name; through Jesus Christ our Lord. *Amen.*

PREVENT us, O Lord, in all our doings with thy most gracious favour, and further us with thy continual help; that in all our works begun, continued, and ended in thee, we may glorify thy holy Name, and finally by thy mercy obtain everlasting life; through Jesus Christ our Lord. *Amen.*

ALMIGHTY God, the fountain of all wisdom, who knowest our necessities before we ask, and our ignorance in asking; We beseech thee to have compassion upon our infirmities; and those things, which for our unworthiness we dare not, and for our blindness we cannot ask, vouchsafe to give us, for the worthiness of thy Son Jesus Christ our Lord. *Amen.*

ALMIGHTY God, who hast promised to hear the petitions of them that ask in thy Son's Name; We beseech thee mercifully to incline thine ears to us that have made now our prayers and supplications unto thee; and grant, that those things, which we have faithfully asked according to thy will, may effectually be obtained, to the relief of our necessity, and to the setting forth of thy glory; through Jesus Christ our Lord. *Amen.*

¶ *Upon the Sundays and other Holy-days (if there be no Communion) shall be said all that is appointed at the Communion, until the end of the general Prayer* [For the whole state of Christ's Church militant here in earth] *together with one or more of these Collects last before rehearsed, concluding with the Blessing.*

¶ *And there shall be no celebration of the Lord's Supper, except there be a convenient number to communicate with the Priest, according to his discretion.*

¶ *And if there be not above twenty persons in the Parish of discretion to receive the Communion; yet there shall be no Communion, except four (or three at the least) communicate with the Priest.*

¶ *And in Cathedral and Collegiate Churches, and Colleges, where there are many Priests and Deacons, they shall all receive the Communion with the Priest every Sunday at the least, except they have a reasonable cause to the contrary.*

¶ *And to take away all occasion of dissention, and superstition, which any person hath or might have concerning the Bread and Wine, it shall suffice that the Bread be such as is usual to be eaten; but the best and purest Wheat Bread that conveniently may be gotten.*

¶ *And if any of the Bread and Wine remain unconsecrated, the Curate shall have it to his own use: but if any remain of that which was consecrated, it shall not be carried out of the Church, but the Priest and such other of the Communicants as he shall then call unto him, shall, immediately after the Blessing, reverently eat and drink the same.*

¶ *The Bread and Wine for the Communion shall be provided by the Curate and the Church-wardens at the charges of the Parish.*

¶ *And note, that every Parishioner shall communicate at the least three times in the year, of which Easter to be one. And yearly at Easter every Parishioner shall reckon with the Parson, Vicar, or Curate, or his or their Deputy or Deputies; and pay to them or him all Ecclesiastical Duties, accustomably due, then and at that time to be paid.*

¶ *After the Divine Service ended, the money given at the Offertory shall be disposed of to such pious and charitable uses, as the Minister and Church-wardens shall think fit. Wherein if they disagree, it shall be disposed of as the Ordinary shall appoint.*

''WHEREAS it is ordained in this Office for the Administration of the Lord's Supper, that the Communicants should receive the same kneeling; (which order is well meant, for a signification of our humble and grateful acknowledgement of the benefits of Christ therein given to all worthy Receivers, and for the avoiding of such profanation and disorder in the holy Communion, as might otherwise ensue;) yet, lest the same kneeling should by any persons, either out of ignorance and infirmity, or out of malice and obstinacy, be misconstrued and depraved; It is hereby declared, That thereby no adoration is intended, or ought to be done, either unto the Sacramental Bread or Wine there bodily received, or unto any Corporal presence of Christ's natural Flesh and Blood. For the Sacramental Bread and Wine remain still in their very natural substances, and therefore may not be adored; (for that were Idolatry, to be abhorred of all faithful Christians;) and the natural Body and Blood of our Saviour Christ are in Heaven, and not here; it being against the truth of Christ's natural Body to be at one time in more places than one.''